The Gift of Loss

The Gift of Loss

By Paula Simon

Copyright ©2010 Paula Simon

ISBN 978-0-557-50924-9

All rights reserved. No part of this book may be reproduced or transmitted in any form or by any means, electronic or mechanical, including photocopying, recording, or by any information storage and retrieval system without written permission from the author.

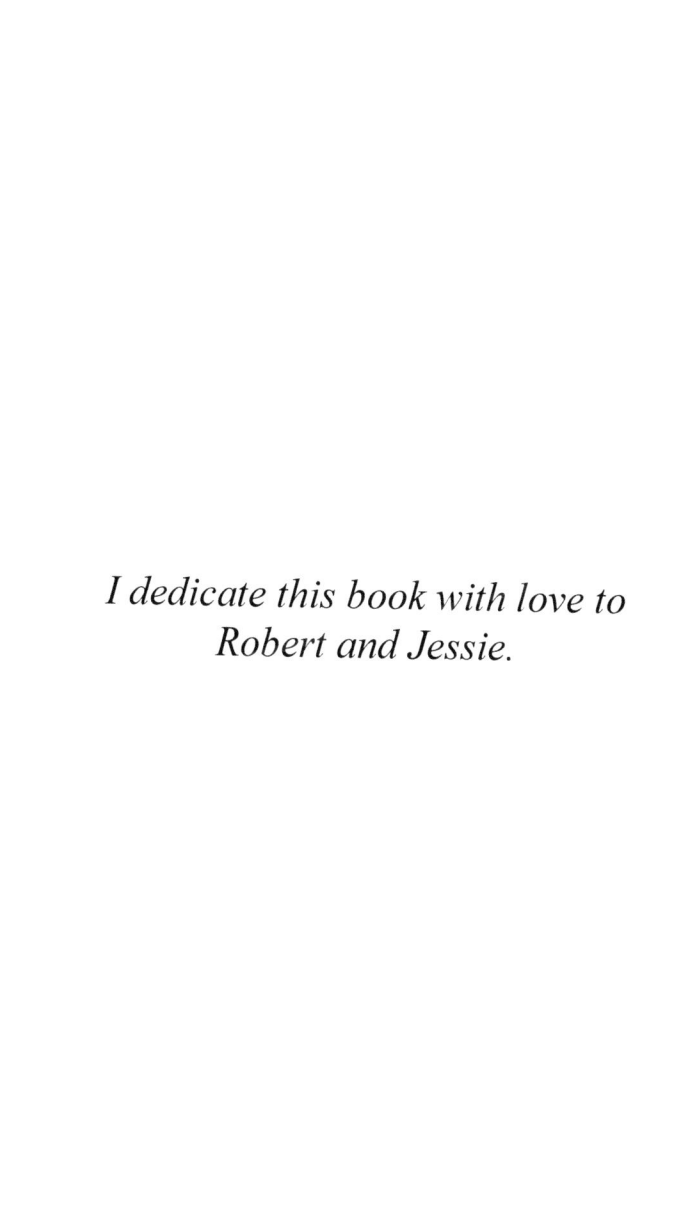

I dedicate this book with love to Robert and Jessie.

Acknowledgements

With Gratitude To:

Robert, whose encouragement, love and belief in me helped me believe I could do this book;

Jessie, for sharing her love with me;

Amy Spurway, for her editorial skills, encouragement and belief in this project. I never would have finished the book without her unwavering support;

Dr. Morry Appelle, for his guidance, insight and wisdom, which created the healing path for us to walk;

Father Denis Costello, who was there to catch us in the hospital as we crashed into the darkness;

Dr. Michael Richler for the kind and gentle care he gave Simon;

Cynthia, Jim, Penny and Michael, our dear friends who gave us unlimited time from their busy lives when we really needed it;

To our family and friends, whose love and support carried us as we traveled on this healing journey.

Contents

Acknowledgements vii

Prologue xi

Part One   Our Story

Pregnant with Possibility 1
A Boy Named Simon..................................7
Ready Or Not 11
The Delivery 17
Simon's First Days....................................19
The NICU Experience..............................22
Homecoming...25
My Son, My Soul......................................29
Back to Work 30
February 33
Saying Goodbye..40
Childless Parents......................................43
Reaching Out 49
Why?...53
Moving On 57
A Whole New Life....................................62
A Girl Named Jessie 66

Part Two   Reflections on Loss

Loss...69
Pain 71
Joy 73

What about God? 74
From Surviving to Thriving 76

Part Three Our Learnings

The Path and the Process 79
Getting Help..80
Taking Time..84
Hard Questions and Simple Answers 87
Routine..89
Flashbacks...90
Preparing For Special Occasions 91
Relationships..93
For Better or For Worse.........................95
Making Big Changes: Let Your Heart
Be Your Guide 97
Advice...100
Simon's Grave 101
Simon's Things.....................................102
Simon's Gifts 103

Prologue

Simon was born on June 6th, 1986. Although he was only five pounds at birth, it didn't take long for that determined little boy of mine to climb to the top of the growth chart. With his olive skin - the kind that would bronze so easily in the summer sun – dark hair, and even deeper, darker eyes that seemed to look knowingly into people's hearts, he had all the makings of a very handsome young man. He might well have hidden his gentle nature in a strong, athletic body, a towering physical presence built to play forward on a hockey team or pitch in the major leagues. His brave heart and sensitive soul might have made him a beloved leader among his peers, especially if he'd inherited his father's knack for putting others' feelings before his own. When I let my imagination run free, that is the Simon I envision. But that is not what the universe had in store for us. Instead, on February 20th, 1987, he died.

So, here I sit in front of my computer, this book being forced out of me. I say forced, not meaning it to be negative. Rather, in an attempt to describe the feeling of being compelled by something beyond my own control to write this book. The feeling is much like what I felt during the years I spent contemplating whether or not to take on a very high-risk pregnancy. Then, there was a relentless need deep inside me that I could not rationalize away. I eventually concluded that I could not grow old without having tried to have a baby, no matter what the consequences. And now, in the face of similar feelings of fear, risk, and uncertainty, I have concluded that I must try to give this book life as well. Another relentless need deep inside that I cannot ignore. I understand all too well that sometimes, you must endure incredible pain in order for something beautiful to be born.

My husband and I are not exceptional people with an extraordinary experience. It is quite the opposite. People suffer unbearable losses every day, and it is that sameness, that essence of the human experience, that compels me to tell our story. I want others who are struggling to cope with a painful loss to know that there are people who understand. And that it is possible to have an even more fulfilling life despite – or even because of – what you've experienced.

This is a simple book. It is the story of our lives before and after the death of our son. Its sole purpose is to reach out and share our story, in the hopes that it might help someone else. Our journey took us from profound joy, to the darkest despair, and into a new way of living in the world. When we were living through our time of overwhelming grief, we searched for inspiration, some sign of hope. It was hard to find. When we were trying to get through the days, weeks and months after Simon's death, I could not see a future worth living. It seemed impossible that life could ever be filled with real joy again. At the same time, I was desperate to find a thread to hold on to. Something to reassure me. Something that would help me make sense of all this pain. I could not fathom that my life could become richer, or that my capacity to feel joy could be restored, let alone be greater than before. But it is.

Loss - and each person's response to it - is a very personal thing. No one can really tell you how you should or should not experience it. It is also not something you ever just 'get over.' Healing does not happen overnight, or without a lot of real work on your self. But you do have one critical choice to make in the face of loss: You can let grief over the loss of someone precious to you destroy you, or you can honour your loved one's legacy, celebrate their existence, and do the work that needs to be done on your own life. My husband and I chose the latter. Very soon after Simon's death, we decided that we wanted to honour his short life by being better people than we were before. We didn't want a legacy of pity and pain. We did not want to be victims of our son's death. It was, and still is a conscious choice.

Having Simon was a precious gift. But losing him was a gift too, albeit a difficult one to receive and accept. May this book help you find the meaning – the gift – within your own loss and life.

Paula Simon

Part One

Our Story

Pregnant with Possibility

Simon was our miracle baby. The baby that neither of us thought would be. I was born with kidney issues that remained undiagnosed until my late teens, and I spent most of my young adulthood aware that pregnancy was probably out of the question. But after Robert and I married in 1980, I began to have more difficulty with the thought of not having children. In 1981, we moved from Halifax to Vancouver. We just packed up and left. The only thing we owned was a 1977 Pontiac Ventura, which we sold for $3000. With that money in our pockets and our minds open to a new adventure, we flew to the West Coast.

My doctor back in Halifax referred me to a specialist at the University of British Columbia about my high blood pressure and kidney issues. For me, it was also a chance to raise the question of having children with a different doctor, with hopes of a different answer. The new doctor said that it was very risky, and that I could be forced to terminate the pregnancy up into the seventh month. She was very clear that if it came down to me or the baby, they would save me. Yet, I was undeterred. Sure, something could go wrong, but everything in life carries an element of risk. Especially the biggest, most worthwhile things, like having a child. I couldn't let fear dictate this decision. It was a chance I was willing to take. Robert, on the other hand, was not the least bit interested in watching me put myself in danger.

So, we tried to adjust to the fact that we were not meant to have children. We had many discussions about getting pregnant, and all of them came down to the fact that Robert felt strongly that I should not put myself at risk. That we should just try to accept this reality. After four years of walking through parks, watching people with their children, and trying to come to terms with our childlessness, I came to a conclusion: I could not accept a childless reality. I could not grow old and look back on my life with that kind of regret. That seemed like a much bigger, more painful risk to me. I had to at least try to have a baby. I had to take the chance. My health was good, but I probably could not wait much longer. After I shared my feelings with Robert, we didn't talk much about it. He knew how strongly I felt, and that there was little likelihood that I'd ever change my mind. And I knew that if it came to a vote, we'd be deadlocked. In the fall of 1984, we moved to Ottawa so Robert could go to Carleton University to do his Masters Degree, and even amidst those changes in our life, my mind remained fixed on one thing: I needed to try to have a child.

In October of '85, Robert headed off to a work-related convention in Winnipeg, where I would join him later in the week. Before I left, I just knew that I was going to get pregnant there. I don't know why I was so sure, but I was. I never mentioned it to Robert because I really didn't want any further discussion on the issue. I was going to get pregnant in Winnipeg. That was that.

Sure enough, within days of that trip, I could feel my body changing. Being absolutely horrible at keeping a secret, I eventually let Robert in on what I thought was happening. Then, a drugstore test confirmed it. I was pregnant! Despite all of the discussions and reservations, we were both thrilled. It was already more than we had ever thought possible. We were filled with hope. I know that Robert was sick with worry, but he did his best to be supportive and encouraging. We would both do anything necessary to keep our baby and me healthy.

When I told my new nephrologist in Ottawa the news, he didn't seem as pleased as we were. Although he attempted to hide it, worry was etched in his face. He referred me to the best high-risk obstetrician in the city. Then it started. I had to see her every week. I was monitored very closely. Our whole lives revolved around this pregnancy, with every week benchmarked by our appointments at the obstetrician's office. Our number one priority was to try to hang on to this baby. Along with all the special challenges - the appointments, the tests, the monitoring, the worry - I also had to deal with the usual experiences of being pregnant. For the first three months, I was so exhausted that I'd come home from work and go directly to bed. Robert would make me whatever my heart desired for dinner, but once I smelled it, I couldn't go near it. So he'd try something else, keeping the doors closed so I wouldn't be able to smell it before I saw it. The fatigue and nausea seemed to last forever. But it was what I had wanted after all. I was going to have a baby. Hopefully.

Nothing compared to the experience of pregnancy. It seemed to make up for all those monthly cramps and soiled panties. It made being a woman make sense. I wanted to wear a sign, announcing *Look at me! I'm special! I'm pregnant!* But I didn't need a sign. I was the size of a billboard. Despite my lack of appetite, I was gaining a lot of weight very quickly, and it wasn't long before no one could miss the fact that I was pregnant. I gained so much weight early on that they thought I might be having twins. Which would have been disastrous, as far as the medical professionals were concerned, given that it was going to be a challenge to keep this pregnancy with just one fetus. But for as long as that question hung in the air, I couldn't help but think that if I could only have one pregnancy, how lucky I'd be to have two babies! This was clearly naïve thinking, and a conscious blindness to the real dangers of my situation, but that's where I was. As it turned out, I was only having one baby, which, of course, was a really good thing. Still, I was so proud of my big belly. All the nice things you hear happening to pregnant women happened to me. People gave me their seats on the bus. Strangers would ask how I was feeling and when I was due. It really felt like I was giving birth to a new member of the community, and they just wanted to know how things were going. It was a very special time for me.

And yet, it was also a time of intense stress. We tried to keep our thoughts focussed on the positives for the most part, but the fears and uncertainties were always lurking. The reality of a high-risk pregnancy was tracking my blood pressure daily, trying to get enough rest, going from one week to the next hoping to get through the tests and the doctor's appointments without landing in the hospital. So, Robert and I were both vigilant about my care. Those appointments were physically and emotionally draining. But each time we left a doctor's visit having escaped the hospital, we felt re-energized.

And we had our post-appointment ritual down pat. Robert would take me home, where I would crawl into bed, while he went to pick up club sandwiches and fries from the greasy spoon down the street. It certainly wasn't the best thing for me to be eating, but it was our weekly celebration, our stress management. It was our taste of normalcy amidst an otherwise far-from-normal experience. Robert would bring the white styrofoam packages upstairs to the bedroom, and he would sit beside me as we stuffed ourselves. After that feast, exhausted, satisfied and relieved that another week had passed without a trip to the hospital admissions department, I'd roll over and sleep away the rest of the afternoon.

A Boy Named Simon

The day we found out that we were having a boy was one of the happiest days of our lives. Not because I wanted a boy. I didn't. Not in the least! I was hoping for a girl. And yet, I was overjoyed when we found out because my happiness actually had nothing to do with the sex of the child. It was all in the *knowing*. Hearing that he was a boy was somehow a validation that this child inside me really did exist. It was his spiritual birth for us. It became him. He had an identity. We could now call him by his name: Simon. We could talk to him and think of him as he might be. I'll never forget lying on the bed in the ultra-sound room, and the technician announcing, "It's a boy." I was caught off guard when I started to cry. I hadn't expected the flood of emotion that came with that news, and I was overwhelmed. It was really true. *We were really having a baby. And it was a boy. A boy named Simon.*

Then, I quickly started to deal with the fact that I was having a boy. *How could that be?* I knew nothing about boys, and as far as I could tell, there was nothing I particularly wanted to know about them. I didn't even like boys. The male of our species, as far as I was concerned, was the bane of woman's existence. I grew up with three sisters. I never played with boys, except for when my cousins from Ontario came to visit. They seemed all right, but I was sure they were exceptions to the unspoken rule that boys were generally loud, rough, messy little creatures. My father and my husband were obviously male, but again, I saw them as exceptions. And sometimes even they could be…well…boys. I knew nothing about hockey or baseball, or any of those boy-type things. *How could this have happened to me? Was this some kind of joke?* I was going to be one of those women I had previously felt sorry for. The ones I used to look at and think, *Oh, it's too bad she had a boy…would have been so much nicer for her if she had a girl. Now she's stuck buying hockey helmets and jockstraps, and freezing her butt off at the rink at 6 a.m. every Saturday morning.* Now that was going to be me! What a shock.

This having a boy thing really rattled me. Didn't men symbolize the repression of women? And therefore, shouldn't women be highly suspicious of their intentions and motives at all times? Wasn't viewing men with a healthy dose of contempt the whole point of feminism? But in the days following the revelation that my baby would be one of *them*, I found myself doing odd things. Like getting on elevators and staring at the man I was sharing the space with, thinking to myself, *He has a mother, and I'm sure she loves her son. Maybe he's not so bad. Maybe I've been too hard on all these guys. I wouldn't want my son treated that way. Maybe I should be nicer to them, out of respect for their mothers.* I slowly began to see the world around me through the eyes of a mother with a male child. This didn't mean that I was going to suddenly fall asleep and forget the systemic inequalities I knew existed, but maybe it was time to find my more tolerant side. Did I even have one? *Maybe it was time to cut the males of our species a little more slack*, I thought. *For the sake of my son.*

As time passed, I began to genuinely embrace the idea of having a boy. Not out of lack of choice, or a sense of resignation, but rather as a mission: To be a mother who would raise her son to be a feminist. To respect the equality of the sexes, and to nurture his sensitive side. I started to believe that feminists having male children was probably the best, if not the only way to really change things. I also thought about how much Robert adored his mother, and how special he was to her. I daydreamed about the relationship I would have with my son. How he would love me for who I was, and how he would always want to be there for me, the way Robert wanted to be there for his mother. How boys always think their mothers are beautiful and special and perfect…even though they hang out with their fathers.

Simon, simply because of his maleness, had already started to radically change the way I saw the world, and how I wanted to be in it. From the moment of his conception, I started to change in ways I never could have imagined. And to this day, he is still having a profound impact on my life.

Ready Or Not

"Simon's moving!" "Simon's sleeping." "How should we decorate Simon's room?" "When should we get Simon's crib?" It brought Robert and I both so much joy to be able to talk about our son. We collected antique pine furniture, and we bought a beautiful armoire on one of our trips back to Nova Scotia. Robert decided to strip and refinish the piece for Simon's room. He put a lot of time and love into it. He made little shelves for his clothes, and we bought a special knob that he put down low so that little Simon could reach the door himself someday. It was truly magnificent when it was finished.

With every passing week that we made it home from the doctor's appointments, our excitement grew. We really started to believe we were going to make it. Simon was growing, and although my feet could only fit into slippers, I felt pretty good. When I hit 32 weeks pregnant, my office had a surprise shower for me. My co-workers were very generous, and everyone was so happy for us. That night, I felt particularly exhausted, and when I got home to do my routine blood pressure, it was very high. We figured that I was overtired, what with all the excitement of the baby shower. Maybe a good night's sleep would bring the morning's reading back into better territory. We hoped.

The next morning's reading was no better. I had a bad feeling that this was it, what we had been trying to avoid. We called the doctor, and she told us to come in. And bring my suitcase. I was terrified, and started to cry. What did this mean? We had come so far, now what? I kept telling myself, *Thirty-two weeks is a viable fetus. Simon will be all right. They told me a baby can survive being born at 28 weeks. We're four weeks past that.* And then another frightened voice would interrupt my self-administered pep talk. *But we're still 8 weeks early! You're going into the hospital! Oh God, what does this all mean?*

I was admitted to the hospital that morning. After lots of tests and many visits from doctors and nurses, it was time to settle in. That first night, Robert stayed until about 11 o'clock. I didn't want him to leave, but there was no place for him to rest, and I had to get some sleep. I walked him to the elevator, and then went back to my room. He could see my room from where he parked so I could wave goodbye to him. And that became our new ritual. Me waving goodbye to him from my hospital room window. Every night after Robert left, I had a little cry for Simon and me.

Robert spent most of every day with me. We got into a routine. Routine really can be a good friend when you are trying to make sense of a difficult situation. Creating your own rituals gives a sense of taking some control back, of claiming a small amount of floor space for your own. We knew that I would be here until Simon was born, and if we were lucky, that was going to be quite a while. So Robert started lugging things for me from home: a radio, a pillow, some of my own dishes, vases for my flowers. And of course, the all-important treats.

I felt more like an inmate than a patient. There was a sense of lost freedom as I tried to go about my days, spending as much time as I could off my feet, knowing that if my vitals didn't 'behave', what little liberty I had would be taken away. I was losing protein, and my blood pressure was not co-operating. Consequently, I had to drag an IV pole with me wherever I went. But even that, you can get used to.

When the purpose of your stay is to rest and relax while the medical professionals try to keep your pregnancy intact, you spend a lot of time talking to yourself, trying to work with them instead of against them. Trying to remain calm. I talked to Simon a lot during that period, too. Trying to keep us working as a team. Telling him that we'd get over this hurdle. Saying things like, "We can do it!", "Together we can beat this!", and "You keep gaining weight like a good boy." The weight gain seemed to be a very important issue to the doctors. Premature babies need as much body fat as possible in order to handle the struggles they often face after birth.

To ensure that Simon would have the best of care after he was born, Robert and I spent time looking for a good paediatrician. The day after I was admitted, we had an appointment to interview a Dr. Richler. Obviously, I couldn't make it to the appointment, so he agreed to come meet us at the hospital. Michael Richler was the kindest soul you would ever want to meet. He was a young paediatrician with a very gentle manner, and I knew immediately that he was the one I wanted to care for Simon. We talked about details: the pros and cons of circumcision, and how once the baby was born, he would come in and immediately oversee his care. He even dropped in to see me in the hospital before I gave birth to Simon, something that I really appreciated.

Time crawled in the hospital. I put myself on a schedule to help me manage the days, and to take back some sense of control over my life, as artificial as that was. I had my morning order of operations: Get up, go to the bathroom, wash my face, brush my teeth, get back in bed, wait for breakfast. Touch base with Robert to fill him in on how my night went, and to see how his day was unfolding. I was lonely. But I tried hard to fight that with my little routine, and with the knowledge that the calmer I stayed, the better it was for Simon. While I waited for my breakfast to come, I'd have a little one-way conversation with the baby in my belly. *Good morning honey! We made it through another night…hmmm what gourmet delights will they be offering us this morning? More scrambled eggs, perhaps? Not to worry. Daddy will bring us whatever we want later.* Then I'd spend some time gazing out the window at the weather, making observations and commenting to myself, to Simon. *Hmmmmm. Looks like it is going to rain. Probably best that we stay put today.* Then I'd take time to savour my tea, and talk to Simon some more. By then, the cleaning staff was starting to come around. I always looked forward to seeing them in the morning, this group of hardworking, mostly immigrant women. They were, by far, kinder to me than anyone else in the hospital.

After breakfast, I'd shower, get dressed, tidy up, and start on Simon's quilt. I had started the quilt years before, and never gotten around to finishing it. When Simon came along, I decided that I would finish it for his crib. I would prop myself up in bed, listen to CBC on my radio, quilt, and talk to Simon until Robert arrived about mid-morning. The doctors would come and go, the nurses were in and out fussing with my IV, and occasionally, I had company. I didn't much like having company in the hospital. There was something about the lack of control over my own privacy that I couldn't stand. If I'd been home, people would have called before coming over, but in here, they just dropped in whenever they felt like it. And I was supposed to be grateful. I wasn't.

The Delivery

Then the morning came. The nurses did their standard blood pressure check and clearly they weren't happy. Shortly after that, the specialist came in and checked me again. With all my indicators taken together, they decided that it was time to deliver the baby. I started to shake. I was terrified. I called Robert and told him to come right away, they were going to take the baby today, and that I was on my way to the delivery room.

Before Robert could get there, they put me in a wheelchair and took me off to another wing of the hospital.

Robert arrived shortly after they'd placed me in a dingy space that looked like something out of M.A.S.H. My blood pressure was climbing, so they put me on a stronger IV drug to try to bring it down. At the same time, they inserted some kind of pills into my vagina in an attempt to help me dilate. My recollection of the next 48 to 72 hours is a little foggy: however, there are some details I will never forget. I remember how the medication made me sick. How the room looked and felt like a nasty little torture chamber. And how, after a full day of extreme discomfort and sheer terror, I heard the doctor say, " She is going downhill really fast. I think we better do a section. Now."

I think I went into some kind of shock or seizure. To this day, I don't really know. It was never really explained to Robert or me, and we had far too much on our minds then, and afterwards to bother asking. I was vomiting and my body had gone from shaking uncontrollably on the gurney, to literally bouncing. By then, Robert had changed into scrubs and entered the delivery room. He stood at my head, holding my hands, trying to help keep my body movements to a minimum. He was in almost as much shock as I was, but if anyone could help calm me down it was Robert. He has always been my anchor, and was the best nurse I have ever had. Trying to be brave, he talked me through it all, giving me as much reassurance as he could through what was a horrifying experience for both of us.

There was a sense of incredible urgency in the room, with a team of doctors and nurses working at a frantic pace. When Simon was born, Robert saw him. Our baby was blue. They wrapped him and rushed him out of the delivery room. It all happened so fast. In that moment, as they rushed Simon out of the room, I remember Robert standing there, caught between not wanting to leave me and wanting to be with our son in the neonatal intensive care unit. I looked at him, and just said, "Go!"

Simon's First Days

I can't even imagine the hell my husband lived for the 48 hours that followed Simon's birth. I don't think he left the hospital for any more than a couple of hours during that time. He was literally running between me – in and out of consciousness, and unable to get out of bed because of my own health crisis - and Simon, our tiny baby struggling to hold on to his life, in the NICU. The baby I had been waiting for had finally been born, but we were both too sick to be together. I found out later that Robert had been taking pictures like crazy. He was afraid that Simon might die before I got the chance to see him.

Robert kept insisting that Simon needed me, and finally, he got me in a wheelchair and pushed me down to the NICU. I'd never been in an NICU before, and I didn't know what to expect. And I was not prepared for what I saw. Nothing can prepare you for the first time you see your baby in that condition. Even the pictures that Robert had shown me didn't ease the shock of reality. My five-pound baby boy lay there, isolated in a hard plastic cage, struggling to breathe. His naked, fragile body pierced with tubes and covered with probes. He looked too small to have so much equipment invading his little body. It looked painful.

The sight of my son flooded me with feelings of helplessness. *How could a child ever recover from such a beginning? What was his little mind thinking? How was he to know that it had to be this way? Did it have to be this way? He needed his mother to hold him and I couldn't get near. All this time we spent together working as a team, and now he was on his own and there was nothing I could do. It was almost unbearable. No child deserved this.* I was so sad. I felt so defeated, and overwhelmed by the fact that there was nothing I could do. Seeing my baby for the first time wasn't supposed to be like this.

Robert wheeled me back to my new room, in a section of the floor set aside for mothers who had delivered their babies. The hospital was sensitive enough to put me in a private room, but all around me were reminders of what I was missing. Hearing the excited voices of families celebrating their new arrivals, and those healthy babies crying, and watching people scurry joyfully up and down the halls was nothing short of devastating for me. My breasts were swollen with milk and aching for my baby to nurse, but he couldn't. My body was tired and longing to be with Simon, but he couldn't be with me. I put on a brave face as my parents ended their visit that night and headed back to Nova Scotia. I even told Robert to go home and get some much-needed sleep. And I cried that whole night. My heart and spirit felt broken. I didn't sleep for a moment. I just sobbed and sobbed. I wondered how I could have been left alone, not even checked on once by the nursing staff, through the entire night. By the morning, my eyes were so swollen that I could hardly see. I was so embarrassed when the doctors came in, because it was obvious what I had been doing all night. It was a little hard to fake it when they asked, "How are ya doing?", not really wanting the details. *Oh great! Just great! How the hell do you think I'm doing?* I wanted to scream. But I didn't.

I remember dwelling on the thought that we'd made it to 36 weeks. The doctors said that a baby could survive being born at 28 weeks. If this was eight weeks beyond that threshold, what could a little soul that was smaller and more premature even look like? Over the next two weeks of our stay in the hospital, that question would be answered, and we would feel blessed by comparison. We would look like the lucky ones. And in so many ways we were. It doesn't take long to realize that it can always be worse.

The NICU Experience

It was time to pick myself up by the bootstraps, and take what little control I had over the situation. Simon needed me, and there were things I could do. I remembered hearing how babies could recognize their mother's voice because they'd been hearing it the entire pregnancy. So, Simon could probably recognize me! I though that if I talked to him, if I sat with him, he would feel my presence and know that I had not abandoned him. Then, a nurse on the floor gave me a breast pump. There was something else I could do. Mother's early milk was full of good things for the baby! So I started to pump my breasts, knowing that when the time came for Simon to have some nourishment, it would be the healing milk from his mother.

Every four hours, I pumped my breasts, carefully labelled the little container and walked it down to the freezer in the intensive care unit. Again, the ritual was very important to me. It made me feel like I could really help. Not to mention the spectacular growth of my tiny 34 AA breasts to 38 Ds. Those breasts that had rested on my belly before I gave birth, and bumped into the sink when I brushed my teeth were now a source of pride and joy because they could help my baby grow. And my husband had no complaints either.

My remaining days at the hospital were spent going back and forth between my room and the neonatal unit. Stopping at the entrance to wash my hands and put on a hospital gown. Sitting at Simon's side, talking to him and watching his naked body through the sides of the incubator. His skin was nearly transparent, irritated and bruised from all the tape and punctures. He was born with a head full of dark brown hair, but as his little veins collapsed, they started to shave parts of it to find good veins for his IV. Little by little, he lost it all except for a small strip on top of his head. I grieved every time they shaved a part of his head. There was something sacred about his head, his hair, that I could not understand but that I certainly felt ever time they made another bald patch. It was a combination of the violation of my baby's lovely hair, and the fear that with each shaved patch, they were one step closer to running out of 'good veins.'

We slowly got used to all the medical equipment around Simon. But there was no getting used to all the poking and prodding of his tiny body. We just had to tolerate it and trust that it had to be done. Simon was making progress, but there were still no guarantees. Every day, we looked for the little indicators that he was improving, that he would be all right. They reduced the level of oxygen in the incubator. The oxygen level in his blood was up. Slowly, slowly, he improved. There were even days of really good news. Like the day he had his first bit of breast milk. It was through a tube that went from the inside of his nose down to his stomach, but he had it, and that was progress. Eating and gaining weight had to happen before he could go home, and the sooner that process began, the sooner he could be with us. Milk from a nasal-gastro tube was the first step.

The day Robert and I walked into the NICU and were told that we could hold him, we felt like kids at Christmas. Who should go first? "You go ahead!" "No you go ahead!" Just to finally have him in our arms was such a relief. To be able to hold him and touch him. It was nerve wracking trying to ensure that we didn't unplug his many wires and tubes, but we got used to that, and the nursing staff was great at reassuring us that it was ok. The next step was breastfeeding, with the nasal tube still in because Simon and I both needed to get acquainted with the process. These were real high points for us. The tiny, precious triumphs that made the rest of it worthwhile.

Homecoming

The day came when I had to leave the hospital without Simon. That was difficult. Still, we spent most of our waking hours at the hospital, and they were good about letting us call to check on Simon any time of the day or night. So, before we turned the light off at night, I would call. If I woke up in the middle of the night, I would call. Otherwise, I'd never be able to get back to sleep. My maternal need to know that my child was ok just took control of me, and that was that.

I remember vividly the day we went to see Simon, and found that they had moved him from an incubator into a bassinet. The kind they put healthy babies in! What a thrill to see him in a sleeper and wrapped up in blankets. Seeing that, we knew it was only a matter of days before he could come home. Once they were satisfied that he was eating well, and once we had learned to bathe, diaper and dress such a wee person, under the watchful eyes of the nursing staff, he could come home. He would finally be 100% ours.

When the day finally came, we could hardly contain our excitement. We brought in all the special 'going home clothes' that had been ready and waiting for Simon for months. Everyone in the nursery was excited for us. It was a success story: a baby was going home. We gave him a bath, and dressed him in his pretty new things that were many sizes too big, but we didn't care. He looked terrific as far as we were concerned. We put him in his 'love bucket' car seat and propped him up with blankets. He looked too tiny to be transported in anything, and we were anxious to just get him home safe and sound. Our baby was coming home. It was a good day! We took lots of pictures.

Things felt pretty normal for a while after that, but then again, what did we know. I was exhausted, still not fully realizing the physical and emotional beating I had taken. Robert went back to work, and all I could accomplish was feeding and changing Simon. During the day, I would lie on the sofa, Simon sleeping soundly on top of me. For weeks, it did not even occur to me that I should try to make dinner, nor did Robert even mention it when he came home from work. Things were going well. I was getting better and Simon was growing like a weed. It seemed like a miracle. Robert and I cherished this baby, who had already been through so much, and we gave him the appropriate title of "King Simon."

In August, Simon landed in the hospital for four more days, this time with a bladder infection. We never left him alone while he was there. I slept beside his crib in a fold-out chair that the hospital had just for that purpose. There was no way I was leaving him. We shared that hospital room with a little girl named Stephanie, who was awaiting a liver transplant. Seeing that little girl and her family really kept our hospitalization in perspective.

Of course, we had no idea then of the ironic twist our lives would take. After that hospital stay, we would have two more contacts with Stephanie's family. Once, on a beautiful spring morning, months after Simon's death, when Stephanie's mother called to invite Simon, Robert and I to the first birthday she never thought her daughter would see. My heart sank when I realized what I had to tell her. The devastating news of Simon's death crushed the excitement in her voice, and in that moment, I wanted to somehow go through the phone and be with her, but there was nothing I could do. The second time we saw her family was that winter, when we attended Stephanie's wake.

My Son, My Soul

I felt such a deep connection with Simon. My feelings were so strong it overwhelmed me. I was not prepared for the depth of my connection with him. It was an experience that I had never known before. There were times when, at night in his room as I stood rocking him in the dark, I could feel his spirit fill my body. Like I was inhaling him. Those moments were overwhelming. I felt as if we were one, like our souls had melted together. A feeling so much stronger than love. I was rattled by the depths of such feelings, and how vulnerable I felt. No other relationship in my life was this powerful. No other human being had this kind of power over me. I felt such gratitude to have him in my life. I wrote poems trying to express how I felt, but they merely touched the surface.

> *My son my soul we are one*
> *Your heart beat and blood runs through my body*
> *You cry and tears fill my eyes*
> *You hurt and I feel pain.*
>
> *My son my soul we are one*
> *With you I am whole*

I see me in your eyes
I feel me in your touch

My son my soul we are one
With you life has meaning
I have been reborn
My son my soul we are one

Later that August, we took Simon home to Nova Scotia to show him off to our families. It was a wonderful trip. We got the chance to be proud parents, and the months that followed were a very blessed time for me, filled with great joy.

Back to Work

In October, I had to go back to work. I struggled to find clothes to fit my new body, and the energy to face the long work days. This also meant that I had to stop, or at the very least cut back on breastfeeding, which I was not looking forward to. To prepare, Robert took on the task of trying to feed Simon bottles while I went for walks. It was agonizing to hear Simon cry, and my heart and my body ached to nurse him. My plan had been to continue breastfeeding in the mornings and at night, but Simon wouldn't hear of it. He refused. It seemed like his way of taking control. For Simon, it was all or nothing.

My first day walking to work, I remember thinking how special I was. *Here I am on the street walking to work just like I used to, looking just like I used to…well, except for the few extra pounds, cleverly disguised with a new wardrobe. But I am not the same. I'm much more important now. I am a mother.* True, to the naked eye, no one could tell that so much about me, as a person, had changed. But I felt like I had a much bigger, more significant life now, and that made everything else shrink in comparison. I felt so good about myself. Simon and I had both made it, and together, we had something that no one could touch. I was so proud of my motherhood.

At the end of that first day, I was exhausted. I thought, *Ok, I did it. I'm a mother, and I went to work. I proved that it is possible. So please don't make me do it again!* Unfortunately, that was not a choice. So I did get up and do it all again. And again. And again. But work never regained the same meaning in my life. My meaning was Simon.

As Christmas approached, excitement mounted. My parents and my sisters were coming to stay with us. After all, Simon was the only grandchild, and everyone wanted to soak in the wonder of his presence at this time of year. Of course, Simon was too young to know what was going on around him, but it was not lost on the adults. He was our Christmas toy, our bundle of joy for the season. We completely indulged ourselves in the celebration, and the house was filled with an overwhelming feeling of love. I remember eagerly anticipating the New Year, and fantasizing about Simon's first birthday in June. *Now that will be a special celebration,* I thought. A day to reflect on where we had come from, and the remarkable fact that we'd survived it all. I imagined how proud I'd be of our joint accomplishment. An invincible team. Excitement pulsed through me as I thought about the future, and our lives together. I found myself sending our Christmas company off with a "See you in June! We're going to have a big birthday party, hope you can make it."

That New Year's Eve, I felt more optimistic than I had ever felt before. We had our baby - a baby we'd once thought impossible. But here he was, and nothing could have made us happier. The future seemed brighter than I had dared to imagine.

February

Monday, February 16th, I got a call at work from Robert, saying that there was something wrong with Simon. He had had a seizure of some sort, and we needed to get him to the hospital. My heart pounding out of my chest with panic, I threw on my coat and raced home. When I got there, Simon seemed ok, but Robert was in high gear. There was a look of fear in his face I will never forget. We jumped in the car and headed to the hospital. Robert told me about Simon's episode, describing how his eyes rolled back and he just went limp.

The days that followed were beyond a nightmare, filled with medical tests and procedures that we tried to understand, sleepless nights, paralysing worry, and our vain attempts to comfort a child who could not be helped. We struggled with the responsibility of parenthood, trying to decide if we should really be allowing our son to go through what appeared to be nothing short of torture. Simon was in a great deal of pain. They'd given him some medication, but it wasn't giving him any relief. And they didn't seem to know what was wrong with him. Maybe a cluster of underdeveloped veins in his brain. Possibly multiple brain tumours. They couldn't tell us anything until tests either ruled out or confirmed something, and there were many tests to be done. On top of that, there was concern that sedating him so much for the battery of tests he needed was creating additional risks.

Here we were, back in the ICU. The pace at which things were moving was incomprehensible. They gave us a room next to the ICU so that we didn't have to leave the hospital. We tried desperately to help. Simon would thrash around in his crib, crying in pain. He was so strong that I could not hold him in that condition, so Robert would try to hold him as he thrashed. Sometimes, for a few minutes, he would collapse from exhaustion and sleep. At one point, the staff suggested that we shouldn't let Simon see us because he was expecting us to help – which we couldn't- and it was just making him more frustrated. That didn't make sense to me. But nothing was making sense to me. Once, we tried standing where he couldn't see us, but he didn't settle down. And the picture of him alone in his condition just didn't sit right with us at all. We were trying to use our best judgement when we really had no idea which way to turn. It was impossible to comprehend what was happening to us, yet we attempted to keep it together because we didn't want to feel like we were abdicating our responsibility for Simon. But this was so far beyond our control. The truth was, we were bystanders. We were watching our lives crumble in front of us.

There was merely an appearance of parental rights and responsibilities at this point. The staff and the doctors were very good at keeping us informed but it was clear that they were in charge of Simon now. The underlying current of the communication was "make yourself comfortable, stay out of our way, and if you don't behave, you're out of here." Early in the ordeal, after a long day of holding Simon down for a series of uncomfortable tests, I remember assertively questioning a specialist who suggested more tests had to be done. I wanted to know the real value of putting my son through all this. The doctor just looked at Robert, and in a condescending tone said, "She needs a break. Best take her for a coffee now." That was the reality of how much input or control we had over the situation. So, we watched our son's tortured face, listened to his frantic cries, and were mere witnesses to his trauma. The sense of helplessness was gut wrenching.

Conversation between Robert and I was right down to the basics. Like in a war zone, or any major crisis, where time is of the essence and debate is uncalled for. Very little needed to be said. One of our exchanges in the coffee shop went like this:

> Me: *Simon could end up very disabled at the end of this.*
>
> Robert nods.
>
> Me: *I don't care. We'll do whatever we have to.*
>
> Robert: *We could move home, where we could get the support we'll need.*
>
> Me: *Right. We'll need support. Ok.*
>
> Robert: *Ok. That's what we'll do.*

Then back to the ICU, with that being the totality of our plan. We knew what we had to do, and we knew we'd be lucky if we even got the chance to do it. The tests and the consultations with doctors went on from Monday until Thursday, when we were informed that Simon was scheduled for surgery on Friday morning for what they thought was an AV malformation in his brain. The doctor explained all the risks as he tried to reassure us. The long list of potential problems that the surgery posed was pitted against the fact that we had no choice. All we could do was hope that it would be ok, try to stay calm, and keep our fears under control.

Friday morning, they sedated Simon in preparation for his surgery. Robert and I sat silent and motionless by his crib, knowing that at any moment, they were going to take him away. The nurse came to tell us it was time. We walked him from the ICU to the doors of the OR. As the door closed, we both collapsed into tears. There was nothing we could do to protect our son. It was an unbearable combination of helplessness, terror, and disbelief.

Then, there was nothing left to do but wait. Hours of waiting. We paced the hospital floors. At one point, we passed a young man cleaning the floors. He appeared to be mentally challenged, and I thought to myself, *That would be ok. If Simon can experience the same level of success as that fellow, we can consider ourselves lucky.* Robert and I spent much of the time in our room, lying on our respective cots in the dark, trying to stay calm. Trying to think positive thoughts. Trying desperately to keep a lid on our fear. Waiting for news. Four hours passed, and we had heard nothing. It wasn't supposed to take more than four hours. Still no news. Then, over an hour later, there was a knock on the door. I opened it to see one of the surgeons standing there. He said it was taking longer than expected because they were having problems with bleeding. My heart sank. That was one of the risks they'd told us about. Simon could bleed to death in the operating room.

I started to pace and pray frantically. *Please God, save our baby. Please God, don't let him die. Please. Oh my God. Please. Oh my God, please don't let him die.* Soon, there were four doctors standing at our door. I don't recall what they said. I just remember dropping to the floor, sobbing, unable to breathe. *He can't be dead! He is our only child! I can't have any more children. No no no he can't be dead.* They tried to explain what happened. I tried to listen. But I could not even process the horrific news itself, let alone the details. Like the fact that the AV malformation had not actually been an AV malformation at all, but a fast growing, complicated brain tumour.

They asked us if we wanted to see him. We were taken to a private room off the ICU. There was a nurse standing by his crib, where his eight-and-a-half month old body lay wrapped in a blanket, his head bandaged from the surgery. I stood at the foot of the crib, Robert at the side, both of us just looking at him. Simon was gone. His body was there, but the spirit that I had held so close to my heart was gone. Forever.

I had already gone into a state of shock. I was not comprehending anything. Tears poured silently down my face and onto my clothes. I watched in disbelief as Robert sobbed over his body. Picking him up and weeping tears of a grief so deep, so unimaginable. The horrifying reality was impossible to believe. I sat in that hospital room for I don't know how long. There was no time. No other world even existed. I sat motionless in a rocking chair, listening to Robert talk to Simon about all the hopes and dreams he had for him. What he wanted to show him. How he wanted to take him fishing, play baseball, tell him stories. Sobbing all the while. Seeing Robert in such pain was paralysing. I just sat and stared, immobilized by his grief, and my own. Weak and hopeless. It felt like my life had come to an end. I couldn't feel anything except an overwhelming emptiness. The essence of my existence was gone, but I had not died. My body was still here, trying to cope with a broken heart and shattered spirit. *How was I supposed to go on from here?* I had no interest in going on. There was no reason. *What else could there be in life for me, a life without my son? What could possibly matter now?*

Saying Goodbye

Simon lay in an open coffin. The quilt that I'd made in the hospital while awaiting his birth was draped over him. His head was wrapped in cloth to cover the marks of the surgery. I'm sure that when people saw him, they were horrified. But for me, his presence was reassuring: an opportunity for me to continue to mother him, to introduce him, to talk about him freely and proudly. Although it was not a conscious behaviour at the time, as I reflect back on it, it's clear that I was hanging on to my last few moments in a role I cherished. At the funeral, I was still a mother doing her best to take care of her son.

We were surrounded by people during the first few days after Simon died. Family came from Nova Scotia and parts of Ontario. My parents had actually arrived a few days before Simon died, although I hadn't seen much of them because I never left the hospital. I couldn't deal with visitors, which I'm sure left everyone feeling very shut out of our life at a time when it seemed like we should need them most. People wanted to help, but their presence was too much for us to handle. Robert and I were so consumed with what was happening, so completely engulfed in the unfolding circumstances, that we were unable to cope with anyone else's pain or questions or even gestures of support. All of it, from our perspective, took physical, emotional and spiritual energy that we just didn't have. I felt like a displaced person, expelled from my life, homeless, shocked, and bewildered. There was no past or future here, only the seconds that ticked by as I stood in my shoes. Our nerves were raw from the uncertainty and horror.

Despite our shock, we were acutely aware of some things. Aware of how the people around us were responding.

Everyone was very supportive of us. No one made any demands…except the hospital, which made us go back and identify Simon's body while we were in the midst of funeral arrangements. Robert did that alone. I was totally lost in myself, and could not bear the thought of going back there for that purpose. Meanwhile, Robert was coping with his grief alone, and still protecting me with such acts of selflessness. He didn't make me go. He didn't make me feel bad about not going. He kept it together when I needed to fall apart, and he saved me from my own self-destructive desires.

People with whom we had not had very close relationships seemed to come to our rescue, and the experience led us to bond, and develop life-long friendships. On the flip side, some of my oldest and dearest friends were simply and conspicuously absent during the days, weeks and months after Simon's death. For their own private reasons, they were unable to deal with or acknowledge our loss. For years, I puzzled over how so many of my friends could have totally ignored this tragedy in our lives. But most of them lived in other places, so maybe that physical distance added a layer of emotional distance too.

Your senses are so raw during times like this that nothing is lost on you. Your mind operates like a non-descript cork bulletin board. You have no feelings, but your thoughts and observations get jotted down, tacked in place, and sit there waiting for your attention at a later date. People have differing abilities to deal with death, sorrow and loss, and when you are at the centre of it, you become a lightning rod for their responses, both good and bad. Not everyone in our life could handle our grief or their own, but for the most part, we were overwhelmed by people's generosity and kindness toward us.

A few days after the funeral, everyone went home. I know some of them felt like they were abandoning us, but in truth, Robert and I needed to be by ourselves again. There was nothing more anyone else could do, and we had no idea what we even needed. So, as everyone left, we turned around to face an empty house, and our broken lives.

Childless Parents

Robert and I were hanging on by our fingernails. Going through the motions of living. I don't think I was able to give

Robert any support because I was completely consumed by my own grief. Still, I remember him helping me, even as I withdrew deeper into my self and my grief. He tried his best to comfort me, but I did not want to live. If I'd been able to convince him to come with me, I certainly wouldn't be here today. But he was all I had left in the world, and I couldn't bear to leave him. Quite literally, I have Robert to thank for the rest of my life.

Three days after the funeral, I called Denis Costello. He was the palliative care priest we met on the day Simon died, and he had helped us with the funeral arrangements. I was desperate. I felt like I was falling off a cliff, and I was terrified of what rock bottom would bring. I knew I needed help. I was panicking. I just didn't know if I could go on.

Denis agreed to see us, and our long journey out of despair began. He was only able to see us a few times before he returned to Ireland, but on that first meeting, as we sat there in silence, unable to speak because our pain was so all-consuming, he said something I'll never forget: *"With a loss of this magnitude, it doesn't go away. You either deal with it now, or deal with it later."* That was the reality. There was no choice. Deal with it now, or deal with it later. I knew I couldn't continue the way I was - hopeless, purposeless, with no future in sight. I was not dead, even though I wished I were. But I knew that unless a car ploughed me down as I crossed the street, or some other tragic miracle took place, I was going to have to wake up and face another day. Again and again and again. I just didn't know how I'd manage to do it.

I canvassed Robert about both of us ending it all. He refused, and I knew I could not do it alone. I felt stuck, and needed to make a decision about how I was going to go on. Robert and I did not want the legacy of our son to be the devastation of our lives and our marriage. Don't get me wrong, we were totally devastated. We knew it was entirely possible for us never to come back from this. But we decided that we were not going to let that happen. We wanted to honour our son by doing whatever we had to do to pull ourselves back together. We loved Simon, and we wanted his memory to be nothing but positive for all those who thought of him. No way did we want anyone saying that Simon's short life was responsible for destroying Robert and me, as individuals and as a couple. It was our unspoken pledge to each other, and to our son, that we would do all the work necessary to become stronger, better people because Simon had come into our lives.

And indeed, the work was so difficult that the idea of honouring Simon and his legacy was, at times, the only thing that compelled us to continue. Most days, it was physically difficult for me to move. My body heavy, and unresponsive. No relief from the feeling of emptiness. Life made no sense. I sobbed. I often went into Simon's room, where an ocean of thoughts and feelings would wash over me. I just wanted to be in his presence. To somehow recapture his smell and touch. To be with him. To feel his weight in my arms. I sat on the floor next to his crib, holding his clothes to my nose trying to smell him. I sat in the rocker where I had nursed him, and tried to recall the sensation. I sat in his room and just stared at the armoire Robert had refinished in anticipation of Simon's arrival. The beautiful golden orange colour that only comes with aged pine and lots of oil. The little shelves Robert had lovingly built for Simon's clothes. The specially placed little doorknob that was meant to let Simon open it all by himself someday. I felt broken. Beyond repair. Inconsolable. No place to go, and no map to get me out of where I was. Not knowing how to go on, and not even wanting to. These were the darkest days.

We went back to work two weeks after Simon's funeral. Not because I wanted to, but because I really had nothing else to do. I was afraid to face people, not knowing what to say. I felt like I didn't know how to be in the world anymore. I was terrified of strangers. They might ask me questions. "Do you have any children?" "Oh, how did he die?" I was afraid of that. How would I get out of those situations? I didn't know how to behave at work either. The last time I had walked to work, I had been filled with optimism and hope. Now I was empty. How would people react to me? Many of them had come to the funeral, but some had not. What do I say? *Good morning? How are you? I'm fine, thanks?* That scared me. *It is not a good morning, and I'm far from fine, thanks*. I talked through my re-entry with Denis, and we rehearsed it. Still, it all overwhelmed me.

My life seemed filled with contradictions, and everything seemed to emphasize my feelings of loss, while torturing me with painful memories and crushed expectations. The sun felt warm on my skin, but left me feeling cold inside. *How dare it be a nice day when my world has fallen apart!* The night sky blossomed with stars while the moon hung, suspended in the sky as it was on the many nights that I'd held Simon in my arms, rocking him to sleep. I used to stand in his room, cradling him as I looked out the window, marvelling at the magic of the darkness and light overhead. The moon used to reassure me, speak directly to me, give me a sense of peace and tranquility. Now, I felt betrayed by the night sky.

I felt persecuted by all that was familiar. I hated to go out. But once I was out, I hated to come home. I felt like we had lost a battle. Our battle to have a child. A battle I thought we'd won. Now, I was missing in action. Seriously wounded. A prisoner in my own life. Yet, the war was far from over. Tired and disillusioned, Robert and I now had to fight on another front. We were fighting for our lives, our marriage, our future, and for Simon's legacy. But this was a private war. A civil war of sorts. The essence of our lives was on the line, and we had battles to wage for the sake of our emotional, mental and spiritual health. The stakes were very high.

Reaching Out

Ultimately, Robert and I reached out for help because we had no idea how to go on, and we needed something – anything – to hang on to. When Denis went back to his native Ireland shortly after we began seeing him, we certainly missed him but we were deeply grateful for the time and care he'd given us. Visiting with him gave us something to hold on to. Denis's departure also led us to a man named Morry. That was when we started doing the real, serious work of putting our life and ourselves back together. We had already decided that we wanted to open up the door that would release our sadness and pain, instead of keeping it hidden and locked away, but we knew we needed someone we could trust to lead us through it. Morry was the one.

We were given Morry's name by a colleague at Robert's work, and even though he came highly recommended, meeting a person you anticipate pouring your heart out to is an anxiety-provoking experience. As

Robert and I worked our way through the downtown Ottawa streets, few words were spoken. We both struggled to keep our nervousness in check.

> *"Do you know where you are going?"*
> *"Yeah, I think so."*
> *"There's the street."*
> *"Yeah, I know."*

We turned the corner into an old, well-established residential neighbourhood that seemed reserved for Ottawa's six-figure folks: Professionals who wanted easy access to the downtown lifestyle, from the comfort of their lovely brick houses and majestic tree-dappled streets. My heart stopped as we approached the street address for Morry's office. We parked across the street from the green, mostly wooden building. Its contemporary edge stood out in contrast to the majestic old trees, and the charming brick homes with their muted accent colours. The building itself looked almost as out-of-place as we felt. Robert and I took a couple of deep breaths as we sunk deeper into our car seats, trying to get a grip on our nerves. We were plenty early. We rolled down the windows and sat quietly, waiting for a few minutes to pass. The heat from the spring sunshine warmed the car. Chirps from hidden birds in the surrounding trees and gusts of fresh spring air helped transform our anxious silence into a calm, peaceful quiet. Finally, we were ready.

We made our way to the second floor, and sat in a little waiting room. Our eyes scanned the place, trying to get a sense of the person we were about to see. A slight, soft-spoken man with warm eyes and a gentle manner came out from behind one of the closed doors to greet us. He smiled and quietly invited us in. I had no idea what to expect, my mind racing with questions. *Could anyone else hear us? Who would speak first? What should we say? What shouldn't we say? Where would we even begin?* Morry quickly made us feel safe, both with him, and with the process we would be undertaking. We entrusted our lives to him. For much of that first year, my life was all about just trying to survive between appointments with Morry. I saw him twice a week alone, and sometimes once a week with Robert.

We started counselling to cope with Simon's death, but we realized after some time had passed that in order to go forward, we were going to have to face all our personal demons: things from our childhoods, our families, and our relationship issues. Everything was going to be put through the wringer. Like everyone else, there was plenty in our lives that was far from perfect, but we'd managed to sweep it all under the carpet. Until Simon's death. Keeping those demons at bay takes a lot of energy, and we were using all of our energy to get through each day. That meant that all kinds of issues were rising to the top, and demanding attention. Nothing was sacred. The good news was that the more we uncovered, the more we invested, and the better off we'd be in the long run. The bad news was that it was really, really hard. We were just overwhelmed by our lives. Caught on a rough sea. No sign of the shore.

After individual sessions with Morry, we each waited with great anticipation for the other's debriefing. *What happened? What did Morry say? How do you feel?* In those little debriefings, and in between sessions, I processed what I was learning from Morry, from myself, and from Robert. The work was intense. It was like a PhD in surviving my own life.

Why?

The work began with the question "Why?" *Why is this happening to us? Why have we been targeted for such cruel punishment? Why, when Simon was the only child we could ever have? Why, after all we'd been through to bring him into the world? Why, when we'd loved him so much, and had never taken him for granted, not even for a moment?*

Why him? Why us? Why me? Why?

That little three-letter question was the most difficult one to ask, let alone answer. And it was where we started in our therapy. It was hard to get beyond it, and it was where much of our pain was generated. The 'whys' of it all were agonizing. It defied understanding. There was no answer. Nothing that could leave us feeling like it had been resolved in any concrete, matter-of-fact way. No eureka moment of "Oh yes! Now I understand!" Instead, we were left to grapple with all the ambivalence, uncertainty and vulnerability we felt.

It was much more than just 'why did this happen?' It was 'why should we go on?' Why bother trying to be good people? Why don't these things happen to people who don't give a damn about anyone else? We weren't about to completely change our entire value system, but we could no longer take it all for granted either. All of these underlying questions needed attention, as everything we had once believed now made us uneasy. We didn't know how to make sense of anything around us. We were not religious people. I had been raised Roman Catholic, and Robert, Baptist, and we did believe in God. But we only attended church at Christmas and Easter. Simon had not been baptized. God and spirituality were not ideas we could quickly and easily turn to. But no amount of talking or reading seemed to help us with the question of 'why' because our reference points were still in the world of the concrete. We needed to move outside of the concrete, and into the spiritual. To explore ideas of a higher being. But that also led us into a great deal of turmoil. *God? What God? What kind of God would do this to good people like us, while plenty of bad people out there would never have to face such pain and sorrow?* We were going through a time of great questioning, with our entire belief system under scrutiny. Could we have been so wrong? Had we been fooling ourselves about the importance of leading a 'good' life? Why did it matter how we chose to be in the world if really bad things could still so easily happen to us? *Why not be completely selfish and consumed by your own life if, at the end of the day, God was going to just hand you the short end of the stick anyway? Otherwise, you're just a fool, aren't you?*

I had a Masters Degree in Social Work, and Robert a Masters in Sociology. Yet, all the analytical abilities we had accumulated gave us no tools to deal with any of this. Up until this point, we had put social justice and working for a better society as high priorities, in terms of how we wanted to conduct ourselves and lead our lives. But all along, we had been subconsciously operating on the assumption that living a 'good' life – being 'good' people – would somehow protect us from really 'bad' things. That assumption was wrong. Now, it was clear to us how naive our notion of the world had been. It's also an assumption that many people unknowingly carry with them. That is, until they are confronted with a tragedy, and find themselves asking that impossible little question: Why?

For us, 'why' was just the beginning of the journey. We had so many questions we needed answered, and we needed something to hold on to. But 'why' wasn't it. We had to let it go, at least for the moment. There were, as it turned out, other more urgent issues on our plate. We had to figure out how to answer other peoples' questions about whether or not we had children. I needed to be able to hear a child cry without being thrown into major anxiety. My dear friend and colleague was dying of cancer in the same hospital complex where Simon died. I really needed to see her, and she needed to see that I was ok, but I was too terrified to set foot in the building. There were some very practical challenges confronting us, beyond the world of 'why.' So we moved on. 'Why' did not go away. It remained in the background, just sitting there, un-addressed. But, I guess we decided to be patient with God for the time being. Maybe he knew something we didn't.

The Quest for Why

> *Why*
> *There is no answer*
> *Why*
> *Cannot be satisfied*
> *Why*

Why me
Why not someone else
Who else
There are no simple answers

Why
Is the wrong question

How
How will I go on from here
How will I choose to live
Will it lock me in a state of bitterness
Or
Will it enable me to reach a deeper understanding
Of
Why

Moving On

Once we had decided that we were going to have a future, and that it was going to be one that honoured our son, we had to just keep going. Although we had made the commitment to be and do better, we had no idea what that would look like. We continued to work on our grief. I'm not even sure when it happened, but at some point, I actually found myself thinking about the future…*in a hopeful way*. There just came a moment when it felt right, and we just seemed to slip into it. We started to look forward. A small corner was turned when we decided to move. When we packed Simon's bedroom, it really felt like the time had come to move out of the townhouse we had been renting. We didn't have the money for a down payment on a house, so my aunt and uncle gave us a loan, and that summer - about four months after Simon died - we started looking for a house. The typical advice that people are so often given after a loss – to not make any big changes until at least a year has passed – was all wrong for us and our circumstances, and we knew it. Our friends were very excited for us, and we felt like it was a step in the right direction. Like we were investing in our future and our relationship. It was something positive. For the first time since Simon's death, it felt like we were building something again, instead of things falling apart.

We found our house around the corner from our best friends' place. It was a very small Tudor stucco home, owned by a woman who had raised her family there and was now alone and ready to move on. She was a kind soul, and I think she was glad a young couple was going to be moving in. The house had a beautiful giant blue spruce tree in the front. It was a centre hall design with all the original dark oak varnish trim. The living room had a fireplace with a ceramic face and a cast iron fire pit. There were small piano windows on either side. All of the main windows had decorative lead glass that added a lot of warmth and charm. Best of all, it had a back deck that was high off the ground overlooking a beautiful back yard surrounded by large old trees. It was one of the most modest of many very grand properties in the neighbourhood, but it was a quiet, private area. We felt very lucky to have landed in such a healing place. This was to be our new home, where we would do much of the work required to start a fresh chapter in our lives.

Having our friends around the corner was no accident. They were a great support to us, and many a night we spent breaking bread with them. It was the right time to have such kind, generous friends in our life, and so close by. Friends that never judged, always had time, and included us in their lives. We really needed that. I am grateful for them, and the gifts of time, patience, love and friendship they gave us.

Most nights I found long and difficult. But in this neighbourhood, I felt safe, so I would go for walks after dark. The night sky slowly became a comfort again, offering me the safety of solitude. Ottawa's winter nights are often cold, crisp and clear. The snow squeaking beneath my feet, the night air cold on my face, I would walk up and down the streets of our new neighbourhood. The snow painted trees and homes glowing in the starry night were so peaceful, and the magic of both darkness and light wrapped around me in a protective blanket. It was so beautiful that my sadness could not overtake the wonder of my surroundings. I walked and cried, quietly releasing my sadness into the night. It was no longer a cry of desperation, but rather of loss and acceptance. It felt so good. Those walks made me feel grateful to be alive. Afterwards, I felt refreshed and exhausted. Tired enough to sleep, which had been the challenge. It was all part of my personal healing process. I walked all winter.

Christmas that year was very quiet. The weeks and days leading up to it were filled with anxiety. How would we get through it? Special occasions quickly threw me back to the first and last time we got to share them with Simon. Robert and I talked about what would be best. Should we put up a tree? Should we go home to Nova Scotia to be with our families? Should we just go away and pretend it isn't even happening? We decided to stay at home, to put up a tree, and to quietly live through Christmas at our own pace. My sister, who was also living in Ontario, came to be with us. That was great, because she had been with us through much of the experience. It felt like she knew how to be with us. We visited with friends in our neighbourhood, and shared Christmas dinner with our closest companions. We spent time reading and going for walks. It was the right decision for us. It helped us make space for our thoughts and feelings. Being at home gave us a safe place to be with our moments of sadness, and at the same time gave us the opportunity to share happy moments with important people in our lives.

Surviving Christmas in one piece was a great relief. We really didn't know how it was going to feel, but the experience of integrating our feelings of missing Simon with the ability to still enjoy moments during the season gave us a little confidence that it was going to be all right. That we would be able to continue with our lives, and live with our loss. The greatest gift we got that Christmas was the knowledge that we could incorporate Simon's life and death into a healthy future. And it would turn out to be a blueprint for surviving many special occasions to come.

A Whole New Life

That Christmas also brought us another gift: the idea that maybe we were ready to think about another child in our lives. Of course, adoption was our only option. After New Years, I called around to some government agencies, and learned that we would not be able to even get on a list for potential parents until one full year after the loss of our child had elapsed. And then, there was no guarantee of how long it would take to find a child for us. Probably a few years.

I didn't want to wait that long to start the lengthy application process, and then just cross my fingers for a few years in the hopes that we'd eventually have a child. Just as I had felt when contemplating Simon's conception, I knew I was ready and I knew I had to try everything in my power to see what would happen. We decided to look into the private adoption route. We contacted a social worker working in private adoptions, and got the ball rolling. For anyone that has been through this you know how much work is involved: home study, reference letters, and a detailing of our family history. We were highly motivated, and completed the process in a couple of months.

After we finished the paperwork, our job was to get the word out that we wanted to adopt. Essentially, it would come down to luck. Or fate, depending on what you believe. So I started telling people about wanting to adopt, meeting with parents who had successfully adopted children, and getting advice as to how to proceed. That was all we could do. Keep talking, follow up with people, let everyone know that we wanted to make a home for another child.

Meanwhile, interesting developments were happening in other areas of our life. Early in the New Year, I received a call from a colleague in Vancouver who wanted me to come out and interview for a senior position with the government. We had moved from Vancouver to Ottawa three years earlier, to be at least a little closer to our family in Ontario and Nova Scotia, but Robert and I thought that maybe a move to

Vancouver would be good. We had friends there, and we enjoyed the west coast. I went out for the interview, and after a couple of weeks, they offered me the job. Although we had started the process of private adoption, every indication was that it would still take years to find a baby. We could continue the quest for a family on the west coast just as easily as in Ottawa. So, after much thought, we decided to make the move back to Vancouver. An exciting professional opportunity seemed like just what I needed. I gave notice at my job in Ottawa. The wheels were turning. Our new life was in motion.

The day we put our house on the market, it happened. We got the call. Our social worker had presented our profile along with a few others to a young woman, and she had chosen us. *A birthmother had chosen us! We were going to have a baby!* An almost unbelievable future lay before us, with a whole new set of circumstances to consider. *What about the move to Vancouver? Did we still want to go? If we did, could I get parental leave before even starting the new job? Did we want to live that far away from family with a new baby, after all that we had been through? Could I take back my resignation from my current job?* Our world was turning at quite a clip, and sorting it all out took some serious thought. I called my upcoming employer in Vancouver, and he didn't make it easy for me. He said whatever I needed, he would arrange. They were committed to women - to mothers - in the workplace, and he felt that my circumstances could be accommodated. Robert said if I really wanted to go, he would leave his job and take on full time childcare. The decision was really mine.

The one thing I knew for sure was that I wanted to be a mother. Simon had taught me that. It was not how I had defined myself in the past, and it was not even really how I saw myself at all. But it was how I felt on the deepest level. I loved being a mother. That was my truth. No job could compare to the feeling I got from mothering a child. Simon awakened that within me, and I knew I needed to have children in my life. The last thing I wanted was to bring a baby home and not be the one to take care of it. I remembered the feeling of going back to work only three months after Simon was born because we needed the money, and I knew I didn't want to do that again. Lesson learned. Decision made.

We immediately took our house off the market. I spoke to my employer, who not only gave me my job back, but also gave me the leave I'd need to care for my new baby. Then, we officially started down the road toward the adoption of our beautiful soon-to-be daughter.

A Girl Named Jessie

Jessie was born on March 30, 1988, a few days after her due date. Born close to Easter, we called her our little bunny. When it came to names, I probably should have named her Joy because that is what she brought to our lives, and what she brings wherever she goes. Right from the start, Jessie was a contrast to Simon in so many ways: From her light brown hair and her flawlessly fair complexion, to the chubby little full-term baby limbs that reassured us - her hyper-vigilant parents - she was healthy. On the day Jessie was born, our world began to turn in a whole new direction. And it has been thus ever since.

I hung pretty pastel-coloured cloth animal figures on the pale yellow walls of the room that would be hers. A white crib was dressed with matching bedding. A white change table with all the fixings was ready to be called into service. A small nursing rocking chair that had belonged to my grandmother waited in the corner. It was the same chair that I had rocked in as a child. The same chair that I'd used to rock Simon to sleep. That chair was filled with wonderful moments and memories for me, and I could hardly wait to curl up in it with my daughter, and create some more.

We spent eleven more months in that little house in Ottawa with Jessie before moving back to Nova Scotia. We wanted our daughter to be surrounded by the love of her extended family, and it was a good move for all of us. Jessie's arrival was a celebration for us, for our family, and for our community. She was, and still is, nothing short of a gift. Simon was born of my body, and I love him dearly. But Jessie was born of my heart, and she is every bit as precious to me. I am grateful to Simon for giving us room in our lives for Jessie, because without his life and death, she would not be with us. And Jessie is clearly meant to be our daughter. She has grown up to be a beautiful, kind, sensitive, gentle and bright young woman. She is ambitious, and demands a high standard of herself. Like her father, she's athletic and driven to be the best at what she does, and anything less is a frustration for her. She strives to live a deeply conscious life and is an insightful spirit. And like me, she walks on the planet with a profound sense of gratitude. She has a passion for animals and is working towards a career in veterinary medicine. We have raised Jessie with the benefit of all the learning and growth that Simon gave us, and she feels a strong connection to him without ever feeling as though she's had to live in his shadow. If anything, she has benefited from the way Simon's life and death illuminated certain aspects of our selves, and our lives. Jessie, too, is part of Simon's legacy: A legacy of hope and love.

Part Two

Reflections on Loss

The hope for the future
The dreams
The wishes
Gone in a moment of darkness

The joy of motherhood
The love of a child
Gone forever

The pain
The sorrow
Leaves no place to rest
Leaves no place to hide
The hope for the future is lost in the past

March 19, 1987

Loss

Loss is a great equalizer among human beings. It crosses all cultures, creeds, and continents. It is deeply entrenched in the human experience. Because it is something to which we can all relate, it can unite us as people. But on an individual level, it can tear us apart.

When we experience a traumatic event in our lives, we are immediately confronted with loss. The loss of hopes, of dreams, of the future as we assumed it would be. Loss makes our world stop. Reality changes, forever. We change forever. In the face of the trauma, every element of our life demands redefining, as our relationships with others change, our daily routines are drastically altered, and we can experience a deep and painful estrangement from who we were. On top of that, from the time we are small children, we are raised to believe that life has some sort of order that we can bank on. That it is all governed by cause and effect, and if we do no wrong, no wrong shall come to us. Our parents teach us that good gets rewarded, while bad gets punished, and even as adults, we desperately want to believe that life can be rationally reduced to some sort of cosmic, karmic merit system. As if life works on the same principle as Santa Claus: Toys to the nice boys and girls, and lumps of coal to the naughty. Then, when life takes a tragic turn, we feel betrayed by our understanding of the world. We feel like the loss we are experiencing must somehow be our own fault, or we chalk it up to 'bad luck.' Even though this renders us ill-equipped and unprepared to deal with the truth and reality of life, it becomes a catchall for our losses and our unhappiness. It's a safe place, until something deeply and profoundly traumatic enough happens to us. Then, we are involuntarily catapulted onto a path of discovery. A challenging, difficult exploration of the true meaning of our lives. At least, that is what happened to us.

Pain

In the weeks and months after Simon's death, I was getting up and going to work every morning. I have no idea how. I just did it. Work had its challenges, but I had my own office where I could hide and everyone basically left me alone. After work, Robert and I would meet, and find some sort of distraction, usually spending time with our friends. Anything to avoid going home. I can't describe the empty feeling I would get when we could not postpone it any longer. As soon as we opened the door, I would burst into sobs, and then collapse on the steps that led to the bedrooms upstairs. Coming home forced me to face the reality of my broken life, and the magnitude of my own pain was unbearable. This went on for months. Once I got started, I was hysterical, and couldn't stop without Robert's help. He would just sit with me, and hug me until I calmed down a little. My grief was so all encompassing that it felt like an out of body experience. It felt like pain had taken over my body. Like it was the only thing alive inside me.

I never thought that pain would end. I felt out of control and completely consumed by it. At first, it was so overwhelming that it scared me. I thought about suicide, just wanting an escape. But as time passed, it became comforting to me. Pain became one of the things that connected me to my deep love for Simon. So I learned to embrace the pain, rather than fear it. I realized that behind that pain was my intense love for my son. The pain became my tool for learning. Pain compelled me to seek help. Pain demanded that I pay attention to life around me. Pain awakened my gratitude. It was that pain that made me aware of all the gifts in my life, and the great potential of my future.

Then, something totally unexpected happened: I started to experience pain-free moments. Those moments grew into hours, days, weeks, and months. Now, when I think of Simon, the first feelings I have are of love for him, and gratitude for having had him in my life. Not pain. I still have moments of deep sorrow, and am very much in touch with the pain of losing him, but those moments are few. The reality is that my love for Simon, along with the intensity of the pain of losing him, has made my life richer. My life with Simon – including his death - has been one of his greatest gifts to me.

Joy

When Simon died, all the joy seemed to be sucked out of our lives in an instant. We didn't expect to ever feel it again. However, we realized as time passed that Simon's memory could bring us more than just pain: it could bring us joy as well. The joy came from an intense feeling of gratitude for having had him in our lives. The wonderful memories he had given us. The pregnancy that I thought I would never experience. The miracle of his birth and his survival. All of the difficulties we'd faced became treasured memories. Simon had given us parenthood, and nothing could take that away from us. Not even pain.

Joy is in the details. It is present in our lives every day, if we choose to be in it. It's in the perfect cup of tea your husband made and served to you. It's in that spontaneous hug from your best friend. It's in the memory of your baby's first real smile. The trick is, you have to be present to receive it. It's not something you can put off, or make up for when it is convenient. It's being there. Putting in the time, and knowing that time, too, is a gift and that it is limited. Joy comes from paying attention to the important details in your life.

What about God?

I remember quite clearly, on the day of Simon's surgery, hoping for a miracle. I have a vivid memory of the moment when we knew Simon was in trouble, begging God to let our son live. *Please God, please God, please God let him live.* Pacing in that small room, sitting, and then pacing some more. Trying to control my panic. Desperately pleading with God, imploring him to save our son.

Do I think God failed us that day? No. I simply did not know what else to do at the time. Although I was raised Roman Catholic, as an adult, church and prayer and God never played a big role in my life. At the time I believed in God but I certainly did not believe in an all-powerful being that hovered over me, controlling my every move and directing my life. Yet in those last few minutes of Simon's life I would have believed in anything if it could have prevented his death.

As with everything else in my life, Simon's death caused me to reflect on what it is I do believe. I've concluded that there is more to our existence than just the physical. I believe that everything – and everyone - is a form of energy. This energy is here before we manifest into our physical bodies, and it lives on after our physical existence passes. I believe this energy is our essence, our soul, and part of the divine within us. The divine is something we express - or don't express - in how we choose to live everyday. The divine is in us, and all around us.

I have faith that everything happens to us for a reason and gives us another opportunity to choose how we want to express our divinity. In times of crisis the pain may not feel like an opportunity. However, that is when we are challenged to go deeper. To release the need for logical answers and realize that pain, along with joy, is part of the human condition. My spiritual practice and challenge comes from the knowledge that it is up to me to tap into the divine spirit that lives within me: To recognize and accept my frailties, and work everyday to do better. To love myself and others as we are, all divine works-in-progress, doing the best we can on any given day when we are confronted with life's many challenges. To live in a state of gratitude for all that life brings my way. This includes all the so-called ups and downs, and remembering that you could not discern one without the other.

To me, God is not the master of my destiny. God is the gift we each possess to live with grace and gratitude.

From Surviving to Thriving

Despite the passage of time, Simon remains an integral part of our lives. He was the catalyst for who we have become as a family, and as individuals. The quality of our relationships, our lives, and our contribution to society would not have been as great if we had not experienced the death of our son. I am eternally grateful for that pregnancy, and for Simon's life with us, yet without question, it was his death that really made Robert and I look at who we were, confront our own demons, and radically change our lives. Having Simon made us happy beyond measure. But losing him made us better people. It is that simple.

Don't get me wrong, when Simon died, Robert and I never looked at each other and said, "Well, what an opportunity we've been given to be better people! How lucky are we? We should be thankful." Never, never, never. That's not how life - and loss - works. It is much more primal than that. It is a matter of survival.

None of it is easy. Losing a child is not something you ever 'get over.' Even as I write this, after many years have passed, I can hardly see the keyboard for the tears. Your experience is always with you, forming who you are and how you relate to the world. But with any loss, if you are to have a future, you have to deal with the pain of the past. To move beyond pain and grief, you must deal with it. The path you take is a choice. Do you forever wander aimlessly down the road of loss and despair until you are so lost in your own darkness that you can't find your way back? Or, do you choose to see and seize the gifts that have been presented to you, and find a path that will lead you toward healing and happiness, even if it is a long and difficult journey? That choice itself is the difference between surviving and thriving.

Part Three

Our Learnings

Along the way, we used many strategies and perspectives – big and small - that truly helped us. What follows is not a recipe. We stumbled along, and in retrospect, this is how we survived our loss and turned Simon's death into his greatest gift to us. Let me be clear: we didn't know any of this at the time. But it might have helped us a little if we had. Maybe some of these ideas, these ways of looking at yourself, your loss, and your life, will help you get through some difficult days.

The Path and the Process

When we had to face our lives again, the first choice that Robert and I made was a critical one: we firmly decided that we didn't want our son's life be marked only by his death, and for his death to be something that destroyed us, as individuals or as a couple. That was an easy decision to make, but it wasn't easy to follow through. It took serious commitment to move forward, particularly for me at times when I didn't want to move at all. Our choice was not always at the forefront of our minds or our behaviour; however, it was the bigger goal we set for ourselves. It consciously and unconsciously informed everything else we did.

I wouldn't want you to think that it is as easy as making the decision to go forward, and that deciding to honour Simon made it all better. It didn't. We just had this thought that somehow, some way, he deserved better from us, and even though we had no idea how we could do that, we held on to the concept. That concept, and the choice to integrate it into our hearts and souls, saved our lives.

Getting Help

We needed an outlet for our real pain, one that was outside of our normal support system. Where our raw emotions could be shared. Where we could be angry, cry in despair, and where we were not expected to put on the show of normal social niceties and public decorum. Family or friends couldn't serve this purpose because they too were suffering some loss. Not as intense as ours, but nonetheless they too were in pain. Family and friends want to help but they don't know how. Our true, raw feelings could not be shared with them because they simply couldn't cope with it all. When people who love you see you in that depth of pain, they want to make it better and they can't, which makes them uncomfortable. Then, you pick up on their discomfort and wind up spending your time trying to make them feel better. Consequently, you are then left without an outlet for your own grief. Such an outlet is an essential part of healing the wounds loss leaves in your heart, your soul, your life.

When Simon died, we felt like we had lost our way in our world, in our community, in our lives and relationships. For the first little while, I was simply overwhelmed. Nothing I did gave me any peace. If I went to bed I cried. If I got up I had nothing I wanted to do, so I sat and cried. If I went out I felt anxious. Which made me cry. Everything tormented me, reminding me of how I felt with Simon, and how he was gone, and how I would never feel that way again. I had nothing to say when people called to check in on us. My own feelings and thoughts scared me. I knew that I was not capable of getting out of this alive without some serious help. I started to panic. I needed professional help and I needed it immediately. So we took that crucial first step, and sought professional conuselling.

One of the concerns I had was that if I opened myself up to share my pain, I would lose myself forever. The pain felt so all encompassing. This felt like a complete breakdown, but it wasn't. I was simply experiencing the loss in all its reality. This was a key for me: experiencing the full intensity of the feelings. The gift of the intensity was it left me no choice but to deal with my pain. Live in it, experience it, process it, and deal with the fall out. There was no hiding. That's why a counsellor I could trust completely and unconditionally was so important.

We found that person in Morry. We saw Morry, at first together and then separately, for over a year, often twice a week. He did more listening than talking, and guided us gently through our grieving process. Morry was our lifeline. Anytime I felt overwhelmed with fear or depression, I knew if I could hold on until the next appointment with Morry, a little bit of the pressure would be lifted and in the process I could see living for another day. Even though I had decided to protect Simon's legacy by being a better person, that goal could often elude me.

Eventually, everything in my life was re-examined in these sessions: my relationships with my family, with Robert, with myself, and how I communicated with people in my life. In order to put me back together, all of my coping skills and my relationships had to be analysed and challenged. There were many moments that the work seemed too hard, too intrusive. It was like I had moved to a new home. All my stuff was packed in boxes, and before my new house could be orderly again, it was going to get a whole lot messier first, as I unpacked, cleaned up and threw out some of the trash I had collected and dragged from one place to another. There would be no wholeness and no real peace in my life until then.

There was no easy way out of this. We knew if we didn't do all the work required we might lose our relationship and ourselves over time. Our relationship seemed to take on even more importance - a higher calling. Saving our collective memory of our son.

We were, after all, the two people that knew him best and without us together, who would be the stewards of his memory? His memory felt bigger and stronger with us together. So we got the professional help we needed to keep us together, mentally, emotionally, and physically.

NOTE: If you are seeing a professional for help, and you are not able to completely share your despair with them, if you are at all concerned about what they might think, or if you are for any reason uncomfortable, then you are seeing the wrong person. This relationship must be one of complete trust. This will be one of the only places other than the privacy of your own home where you can truly be real with your feelings, so it is important to feel safe and comfortable with the person guiding you through it. This person also needs to have the wisdom to help you process your grief and explore anything else that comes up. Believe me, if you are doing the work that needs to be done, lots will come up.

Taking Time

People said to me, and you'll probably hear it too: "Time heals all wounds." Or

"Life goes on." These clichés only made me feel even more misunderstood and isolated from the living world. Of course, it was in short order that people would then feel that enough time had passed. That it was time for us to move on. Get on with our lives. Put the past behind us. Stop feeling sorry for ourselves. Certainly, if these phrases were not used directly, they were insinuated. I felt like people were looking at me thinking, "She's in big trouble. She isn't getting over this the way she should."

In fact, much is healed with time. Memory fades, and the coarser edges of our grief do get smoother. However, there are two challenges that we faced with this very pervasive way of thinking. With time, our memory of the pain was going to fade but I was afraid as the pain faded, so too would my intense love, and the memory of my son. Secondly, I knew that the quality of the "healed wounds" was going to depend on the work I was willing to do. Time itself may well heal the wounds, but without proper care and attention, they can still leave terrible scars. It is the difference between thriving and surviving. Our commitment to honouring Simon's legacy made Robert and me want to make sure that we would go beyond just surviving.

I really had no idea how this healing was going to happen because it appeared to be in direct conflict with my concern about losing more of Simon if I let go of my grief. It was like I had suffered an amputation. The question was: *Am I going to do what needs to be done? Get a prosthesis that lets me walk and run again, or will I limp painfully through the rest of my life?* At first, every minute was excruciating.

Time was really important on many fronts. We did not want to be pressured by other people's notion of an appropriate amount of time to heal, go back to work, clean out Simon's room, have fun, stay in, or go out. Everyone had an opinion on how long it should take us to do everything, and whether we were doing it too quickly or too slowly. What we came to know was that the only right time to do anything was when we felt ready to do it. For some things, it was sooner than people might expect and for others it was longer. When it came to packing up Simon's room, the right time wasn't until the seasons changed. Simon died in February, and on a warm summer day I walked into his room and saw the winter blankets in his crib. I thought *that's not right. It's no longer cold. His bed needs to be changed.* And at that moment, I was ready not to simply change his bed, but to dismantle it. I was then able to start the process of packing up his room. Until that point, I had still been using his room to feel some comfort and connectedness with him.

We didn't set a month or a number of weeks for when we'd do or not do anything. We waited until each step, each decision felt right to us, and we gave ourselves the gift of time. And because we waited until we were ready, none of the things we did really felt all that hard to do.

Hard Questions and Simple Answers

Robert and I had to do a lot of thinking ahead in order to feel ready to face some days. Before I could handle leaving the house, I had to deal with my fear of people asking me very ordinary questions. Normal questions that I no longer felt equipped to cope with. "How are you today?" "How are you feeling?" "Do you have children?" That was a big one. If I said yes, then they might ask, "How old?" *Then what would I say? Is he the age he was when he died, or does he even have an age now that he is dead?* I didn't even want to get into it. *But if I don't get into it, am I denying he ever existed?* I was really terrified of these questions. Morry helped us figure out what kinds of responses we could be comfortable with. I learned that I didn't owe strangers my entire life story. I only needed to answer what I felt comfortable answering. And to other peoples' inquiry as to whether or not I had children, a simple "no" would stop all subsequent questions if I didn't want to talk about Simon with them. Morry taught me that "no" was not a denial of Simon. It was just a safe place for me, and it opened a path for me to go out into the world.

As for the other questions like, "How are you?" and "How are you feeling?", fake it until you make it. No one is really ready to cope with the true answers to these questions. Most of the time, they are asked in the context of simple social politeness, and a simple superficial response of "fine" is all anyone is looking for. Even when the question is being asked by genuinely concerned friends and family, they are likely not ready for the truth either. And we didn't always want to get into the hard truth with those closest to us. We kept those feeling within the confines of our own private conversations at home, and for our time with Morry. Places where we knew it was safe to express them.

Routine

Going back to work was very difficult but also very important because it gave us some routine. A routine that put us out of the house, and out in the world. At first I felt very distracted at work, thinking constantly about Simon. However, there were moments with my colleagues and moments while doing my job that I didn't think about Simon. There were even seconds when the pain wasn't there either. Those moments were a welcomed relief from how I felt most of the time. Those moments grew in length at work, and while I was away from home. I felt like I was pretending to be ok, and pretending was giving me a bit of an escape from my reality.

Because being out became easier than going home, Robert and I looked for ways to stay away from home. Our reality felt too overwhelming to face. We would meet after work and go out for dinner. We spent a lot of time with friends - friends who understood our need to be out, and gave up much of their family time to keep us company. This is one of the ways we slowly started to get back on our feet. In some respects, it allowed us to indulge in a little bit of denial of our loss and the enormous pain we were in. But it also demonstrated to us that it was possible to laugh and enjoy ourselves again. Still, we felt like we were just trying to survive, and doing what we could to get through one day at a time. At that point, that really was the goal: Survival. Thriving would come much later. The comforting, busy routine we created with work and friends opened the window and let a little fresh air into our lives.

Flashbacks

For a while, I was living with continuous flashbacks of moments in the hospital and of Simon's funeral. They came automatically. I had no control over them, and these flashbacks would drive me deeply into feelings of loss and sadness. I learned that they too were part of my healing process. They were not to be feared, but rather, embraced. The more I relived my experience, the less frightening it became. Reliving these most difficult moments and days became part of the process of integrating this experience into the fabric of my life. Eventually they came less often, and carried with them far less emotion and fear.

Preparing For Special Occasions

During the first year, and when needed in subsequent years, we prepared for special days in advance. We needed to bring some mindfulness to our lives, and to acknowledge that these days might upset us. We needed to talk to each other beforehand to check out how the other was feeling about the upcoming event, and decide together how we wanted to handle the occasion. This was particularly true for the first year. Simon died in February, just after Valentine's Day. Then, we had Easter, Mother's Day, Father's Day, Simon's birthday in June, my birthday and our anniversary in July, Robert's birthday in August, Christmas, New Year's, Valentines, and of course the anniversary of his death to live through. These occasions were so difficult because we had such big plans for the future with Simon. New Year's Eve really stood out for me. Before Simon died, I had been so filled with excitement and hope for the future that I could hardly contain myself. I had never felt such optimism. We were going into the New Year with our little miracle baby and I was already fantasizing about his birthday, and Mother's Day, and how I wanted to celebrate. Then, a month and a half after New Year's, he was gone. For a while, the loss of Simon took away my ability to think about the future or to dare to be hopeful. It took me many years to stop fearing the turning of the year. There was always a little part of me that was terrified of what might be coming.

There was no magic to getting through these days. We just did our best to be in touch with our feelings and plan for the fact that our loss would feel more heightened at these times. This simple mindfulness really seemed to help. As each occasion approached, we chatted about how we were feeling and our anxieties about the day. *Did we want to be with other people? If so, who? What did we want to do? And how were we going to honour Simon's memory on that day?* We needed to give ourselves time apart and time together, to really be in touch with our feelings for Simon on those days. Building in such time as we needed it, and acknowledging that special occasions may hold some difficult moments gave us the strength to face them together. It helped us feel more in control of the day, rather than feeling lost and disoriented in our grief.

Relationships

Simon's death changed everything, even our relationships. Some of my dearest friends - whom I'd stayed in touch with even though we lived in different cities - seemed to just vanish completely during this time in our lives. I don't know if they just didn't get what was happening to us, or if somehow the geographic distance between us made them feel too far removed, and therefore not needed. It was puzzling at the time.

I also remember the various strange reactions other people had in our presence. Some were terrified to see us. They simply didn't know what to say or do, so they avoided any contact with us. I had people go as far as to cross the street to avoid coming face to face with me. What people seem to misunderstand is that there is nothing they can say or do to really make you feel any worse than you already feel. Somehow, people think if they say they are sorry about your loss, that the words will just remind you of it. But our loss was always with us. It was - and still is - an intricate part of who we are. Acknowledging our loss was a loving gesture to us, and was always received with kindness.

On the other side of the coin, people who had been mere acquaintances became our really good friends. Somehow, our loss brought out the best in them, and their unconditional kindness and generosity became part of what made our healing possible. The love and support of other people really can make a difference.

It is probably no coincidence that the two couples that helped pull us through this time had babies around the same age as Simon. Contrary to what many people would expect, it was great for us to be around children Simon's age. It allowed me to meet some of my maternal needs with these children. I know it had to be hard for our friends, and they travelled those uncharted waters with us. They gave us their company, welcomed us into their homes, and allowed us to play with their kids. In return, on occasion we were happy to give them a "worthy" excuse for getting out of other engagements they wanted to avoid. We would laugh together, saying, "No better excuse to get out of another commitment than spending time with the bereaved!"

For Better or For Worse

Without Robert's support, I am sure I wouldn't be here today. Over the first couple of months there were moments when all I wanted to do was end the pain, but I didn't want to leave Robert. Occasionally, in moments of deep despair, I would make the suggestion that we end it all together. He wouldn't hear of it, and so I would crawl back into my hole wondering how I was ever going to feel better. I don't know how Robert got his strength at those moments. I am eternally grateful that he did.

As a couple, you share the memory and the loss together. But choosing to do the hard work of healing and recovery is an individual decision. You cannot make someone else - not even your partner - do the tough work that lies ahead. Robert could not save me from this loss. I had to save myself, and as much as we needed the support of one another along with professional help, we also recognized that the real help and healing had to come from within. I know Robert and I came out the other side because we both committed to our guided self-healing. I do not mean self-help groups, or a mountain of self-help books, although they too can have a place in the process. I mean intensive individual therapy. The term "self-healing" refers to the fact that we were the ones who had to make the changes in our lives, with the therapist as our guide on the journey. The therapist could not make us do anything, and we could not make each other do anything. We participated in intensive therapy sessions over many months. During this process of healing, we found that we had to deal with all kinds of issues because the grief had ripped our hearts wide open. Then, all the other losses, regrets, and hurts came pouring out. At first, it was a bit of a shock that our whole lives and all of our relations were laid out on the table like that. But the insight and self-awareness gained through the work put us on a new life path. It transformed our lives and how we saw the world forever. And over time, it became the foundation of my belief that Simon's death was as great a gift to us as his life. Our dedication to this difficult work saved our lives and our marriage.

We also gave each other permission to feel sad, and to express those feelings at any time. We gave each other space to be alone with our thoughts and feelings if that was what we wanted. We stopped trying to rescue each other from our loss, and accepted each other for who and where we were at any given time. We began to understand that although we had both lost our son, our individual experiences of the loss were very different and extremely personal. We worked to understand how to support each other as we moved through the process of grieving. This is how our marriage survived such a catastrophic loss.

Making Big Changes: Let Your Heart Be Your Guide

The commonly held wisdom on change after loss is that you should not make any major changes in your life for a year. Don't move. Don't make any major purchases. Don't make any major decisions. I don't know who came up with that timeline. It may be a good general guide, and it may be best for some people. For us, it was not something we took into consideration. We made some really major changes, and they felt right.

Shortly after Simon's death, we bought a new car. We'd been making do with an old one that we couldn't afford to replace, but once we found ourselves no longer needing to pay for childcare, we decided to treat ourselves to a new car. It was a great decision. We spent a lot of time in that car in the first months because we didn't like being at home. It didn't take any of the pain away. It didn't replace Simon in the slightest. It wasn't part of our healing. It just was a little bit of physical comfort when there was no emotional or psychological comfort to be found.

Within six months of Simon's death, we also purchased our first home. Not only did it feel like the right decision, but it was also healing on many levels. It moved us out of a dwelling that felt forever grief stricken, and it gave us new, beautiful surroundings that promoted our healing. And it reinforced that life was going to move forward. That move was truly a good thing for us.

And then there was our beautiful daughter Jessie. We started the adoption process less than a year after Simon's death. This timing was "too soon" according to government adoption guidelines. But it was clearly the right time for us. Never did we see adoption as a replacement for our son. There was no replacing Simon. Our intent was to grow our family and have a second child. We had been receiving intensive therapy, and had worked hard to be well again. We knew the feelings and love we had for Simon would not limit us when it came to loving another child. We were ready, and we knew it. Jessie came into our life at the perfect time.

The ability to love and heal your heart is not a science, and it does not adhere to anyone's timeline. Some healing happens quickly. Some takes much longer. Only you know when you are there, and you have to be completely honest with yourself.

For judgmental onlookers, these may have all seemed like highly questionable decisions. For us, we never regretted any of those choices. Maybe because we really front-loaded our therapeutic work, we progressed more quickly. I really don't know. Each big decision we made just felt like a natural progression. I do believe that it came down to listening to our own hearts, and not worrying about what other people thought we should or should not do.

Advice

Through this process, I also learned that the road to hell is indeed paved with good intentions…and that other people's good intentions can create a lot of that pavement. There is no shortage of opinions on what you should be doing, feeling, thinking and believing, and all of the opinions and advice are given in the hopes of helping. The problem for us was that no one could possibly know or understand what was going to work for us.

When taken to heart, much of the advice others offered us could - and sometimes did - make us second-guess what we were doing at any particular time. That advice didn't help us. It created more anxiety. So, very quickly, we learned to be polite when people expressed their opinions, and then just let them quickly flow by us, refusing to be subjected to anyone's judgment other than our own. We learned to trust our feelings when making decisions, and to be comfortable with that trust. That helped us avoid being heavily influenced by what other people thought was best for us. It was a life lesson. And like many life lessons, it was easier said than done.

Simon's Grave

Simon was cremated and his ashes buried in a plot where Robert's parents would eventually be laid to rest. It is an impeccably kept country cemetery full of large old trees, in Nova Scotia's Annapolis Valley where Robert was born and raised. As cemeteries go, it is a beautiful place. Yet I have never felt the need to go there. For me, it is a marker of where his ashes lie, but he is not there. This is a very personal feeling, and one that others may not share. My sense is that Simon is always with me. I feel him with me, particularly on special occasions. When I want to spend a quiet moment with just him, I have no need to travel to the cemetery. I just take that moment wherever I am at the time. I have visited his gravesite and I know that it is well kept, but it does not bring me any closer to him. I feel much closer to him in my daily life than I do at the cemetery.

Simon's Things

The process of knowing what to do with Simon's things came in stages. For quite a while, we left his room as it was, and when we felt ready we packed it. I kept some of his clothing, his special blankets, a few toys that he loved, and his books. His crib, we kept and stored. It would later become Jessie's new bed. Most of the furnishings in his room were antiques that we had adapted into baby furniture, so we integrated them into the rest of our home when we moved. The armoire that Robert had refinished for his closet became a china cabinet in our dining room. I love having it there because every time I touch the child-level ceramic knob that Robert so carefully placed, I think of Simon. It was another positive way of integrating Simon into our daily lives.

To this day, we keep a couple of Simon's photos with the rest of our family pictures. After all, he is still a part of our family. There is one picture in particular that still gives me pause. It was taken when we brought Simon home to Nova Scotia to show him off to our friends and family. In it, I'm standing next to my grandmother, who is holding Simon. I look at that picture and know that they are together in some other realm, but it also takes me back to how happy we were that day. Looking at Simon's pictures puts me in touch with the deep love I have for him.

Simon's Gifts

Simon's impact on our lives is ongoing. As any parent will tell you, your children have the power to send your entire life whirling off in directions you never could have imagined. That couldn't be more true of our life with Simon. We never could have imagined all the incredible things his life and his death would ultimately give us.

Simon's conception gave me the gift of hope for the future. It began my life of gratitude because every step of the way was further than I had ever dreamed possible. The fact that he was even conceived awakened so much hope in me.

Simon gave me the gift of experiencing pregnancy. It was an enormous privilege to carry his body and soul in mine. It gave me the opportunity to see the world through the eyes of a mother-to-be. To share in other people's excitement, and the anticipation of a new baby. To feel life inside of me, and to have my perspective profoundly altered by a person who wasn't even born yet. I am forever grateful for that experience.

Simon gave me Motherhood. I experienced for the first time the depth and intensity of a mother's love and relationship with her child. It was – and still is – a love like no other. I was overwhelmed with the power of that connection. Motherhood took me outside of myself, and sometimes outside of my body.

Simon's death gave me a first-hand understanding of the depths of human suffering and despair, and showed me the incredible strength and resiliency of my spirit.

Simon's life, his death, and his spirit gave me the gift of gratitude and appreciation for every day. He taught me that everything is a gift in your life, if you choose to see it as such. He taught me that at the heart of any tragic situation lay an opportunity to be and do better.

Simon gave me the gift of this story, and the strength to share it with others who might be ready to receive the precious and brilliant gifts that can be found, even in the depths and darkness of loss.

Thank you, Simon.